First Facts®

Who Lived Here?

PLAINS
Communities
PAST and PRESENT

by Megan O'Hara

Consultant:
Zoe Burkholder, PhD
Assistant Professor, College of Education
and Human Services
Montclair State University
Montclair, New Jersey

CAPSTONE PRESS
a capstone imprint

First Facts are published by Capstone Press,
1710 Roe Crest Drive, North Mankato, Minnesota 56003
www.capstonepub.com

Library of Congress Cataloging-in-Publication Data
Cataloging information on file with the Library of Congress.
978-1-4765-4061-0 (library binding)
978-1-4765-5143-2 (paperback)
978-1-4765-5996-4 (eBook PDF)

Editorial Credits
Brenda Haugen, editor; Juliette Peters, designer; Svetlana Zhurkin,
media researcher; Charmaine Whitman, production specialist

Photo Credits
Alamy: North Wind Picture Archives, 7, 9; Library of Congress,
11, 13, 15, 17; National Geographic Creative: W. Langdon Kihn, 5;
Shutterstock: Brian A. Jackson, 20, Lee Prince, 21, Max Voran, 19,
Michael J. Walters, cover (left), Samiah Samin (background), cover
and throughout, Spirit of America, cover (middle back), 1, 2, 23, 24

Printed in the United States of America in North Mankato, Minnesota.
092013   007771CGS14

TABLE OF CONTENTS

THE FIRST PEOPLE ON THE PLAINS

8500 BC TO 3500 BC

THE GREAT PLAINS

CANADA

MONTANA

NORTH DAKOTA

SOUTH DAKOTA

WYOMING

NEBRASKA

COLORADO

KANSAS

OKLAHOMA

NEW MEXICO

TEXAS

MEXICO

People have lived on the Great Plains of North America for more than 10,000 years. Early people lived in groups and hunted together. They hunted deer, elk, and smaller animals.

They also hunted large animals such as bison. To kill the bison, the hunters formed huge **funnels** called bison jumps. The jumps led **stampeding** bison over **cliffs**. Natural objects such as rocks and trees sometimes formed the jumps. The jumps could also be formed using people.

American Indians form a bison jump.

funnel—a cone shape with an opening at each end

stampede—when a group of animals makes a sudden, wild rush in one direction, usually because something has frightened them

cliff—a high, steep rock face

AMERICAN INDIAN LIFE

AD 1600

American Indian **tribes** made their homes by rivers that flowed through the Plains. They lived in houses made from mud that was packed together and then dried.

THE GREAT PLAINS OF LONG AGO

For thousands of years, the Great Plains was a sea of grass. Tall grass **prairies** waved in the wind.

The Great Plains was mostly flat and dry. Trees were rare and mainly grew along rivers. Winters were cold and harsh. Summers were hot and dry.

Today the weather on the Plains can still be harsh. Areas of prairies still exist. But much of the land is now farms, ranches, small towns, and cities.

prairie—a large area of flat or rolling grassland with few or no trees

an American Indian home made from mud

Men hunted bison and other animals.
Women dried the meat in the sun.
This process made the meat last longer.
Women also grew vegetables such as corn,
squash, and beans.

tribe—a group of people who share the same
ancestors, customs, and laws

HORSES MAKE LIFE EASIER
1700s

European traders brought new goods to the Plains. People traded shells, beads, and tools. Spanish traders brought horses. Horses allowed people on the Plains to travel faster. Horses also helped them hunt fast animals.

American Indian tribes moved often to hunt for food. They galloped on horses chasing huge **herds** of bison. They shot arrows at the bison to kill them. They used the bison skins to make **tepees**. The bison's thick fur made warm blankets.

> **FACT**
> When they were around 10 years old, American Indian boys were taught to hunt bison with bows and arrows.

American Indians lived in tepees on the Plains.

herd—a large group of animals that lives and moves together

tepee—a cone-shaped tent used by the Plains Indians that was made of bison hide and tall poles

THE OREGON TRAIL

Covered wagons brought people from the eastern United States to the Plains in the mid-1800s. The travelers used the Oregon Trail. The trail was created by fur traders and trappers. Those looking for land of their own followed the trail through the Plains. Some went all the way to Oregon. Others found homes on the Great Plains.

FACT

The Oregon Trail stretched for more than 2,000 miles (3,219 kilometers). More than 350,000 travelers used the Oregon Trail between 1841 and 1866.

A family stops for the night along the Oregon Trail.

RAILROADS BRING MORE PEOPLE

1850 TO 1900

Railroad tracks were laid across the Great Plains in the 1800s. The trains carried many visitors and hunters. They wanted to see the grassy prairies and hunt bison.

Immigrants also came on the trains. Many of them had heard stories about the **rich** soil. Many immigrants became farmers, growing wheat and corn.

immigrant—a person who leaves one country and settles in another

rich—having many nutrients to help plants grow

Hunters shoot bison that are blocking a train's route.

RAISING THEIR OWN FOOD

LATE 1800s AND EARLY 1900s

People **plowed** the prairie and built **sod** houses in the late 1800s and early 1900s. Farmers grew all of their own food. They raised cows for meat and milk. Women often raised chickens and gathered their eggs. They made butter and baked bread.

Life on the Great Plains was hard. Farmers often fought huge numbers of grasshoppers that filled the sky. The insects ate the crops.

---

plow—to remove or push aside

sod—the top layer of soil and the grass attached to it

A Plains family stands outside their sod home in 1886.

THE DUST BOWL
1930 TO 1938

The Great Plains suffered a **drought** in the 1930s. Crops would not grow without rain. Cattle starved in the dry, cracked **pastures**. Winds blew soil for miles. The Great Plains became known as the Dust Bowl.

BLACK BLIZZARDS

Black blizzards were huge dust storms that struck the Great Plains during the Dust Bowl. The massive storms killed people and animals that could not find protection. The dust was so thick that those caught in the storms could not breathe. The storms created piles of dust that sometimes buried vehicles and small buildings.

A large dirt pile forms near a farmer's barn in Kansas in 1936.

Without crops and cattle to sell, farm families struggled to survive. Many farmers left the Plains to find work in other places.

drought—when the land is dry because of too little rain

pasture—land where animals eat and exercise

BIG FARMS AND RANCHES
1950 TO 2000

The large open spaces and flat land of the Great Plains were perfect for farms and ranches. Big tractors and other modern farm equipment allowed farmers and ranchers to work large areas of land.

Farmers grew a variety of crops and raised different animals throughout the plains. The food the farmers and ranchers produced was sold around the world.

FACT

Many Iowa farmers raise corn, soybeans, and pigs. Farmers often grow wheat in Kansas. Sheep and cattle graze on big ranches in Texas and Oklahoma.

Modern equipment allows farmers to work larger pieces of land.

FARMING AND ENERGY

— 2000s —

Today some farms harness energy from the strong winds that blow across the plains. These farms have huge wind **turbines** that make electricity.

Farmers continue to grow many crops, such as wheat and corn. Ranchers raise cattle and other animals. Many people also live and work in cities or small towns. They work in a variety of jobs, including **tourism**. Many people enjoy the beautiful landscape.

turbine—device with curved blades connected to a central shaft that spins as wind passes over the blades

tourism—the business of taking care of visitors to a country or place

The American bison is a huge animal. It stands up to 6.5 feet (2 meters) tall at the shoulder and can weigh more than 1 ton (0.9 metric ton).

Despite their massive size, bison are fast. They can run up to 40 miles (64 km) per hour. That's only about 10 miles (16 km) per hour slower than the top speed of a horse!

GLOSSARY

cliff (KLIF)—a high, steep rock face

drought (DROUT)—when the land is dry because of too little rain

funnel (FUHN-uhl)—a cone shape with an opening at each end

herd (HURD)—a large group of animals that lives and moves together

immigrant (IM-uh-gruhnt)—a person who leaves one country and settles in another

pasture (PASS-chur)—land where animals eat and exercise

plow (PLOW)—to remove or push aside

prairie (PRAIR-ee)—a large area of flat or rolling grassland with few or no trees

rich (RICH)—having many nutrients to help plants grow

sod (SOD)—the top layer of soil and the grass attached to it

stampede (stam-PEED)—when a group of animals makes a sudden, wild rush in one direction, usually because something has frightened them

tepee (TEE-pee)—a cone-shaped tent used by the Plains Indians that was made of bison hide and tall poles

tourism (TOOR-i-zuhm)—the business of taking care of visitors to a country or place

tribe (TRYB)—a group of people who share the same ancestors, customs, and laws

turbine (TUR-bine)—device with curved blades connected to a central shaft that spins as wind passes over the blades

READ MORE

Bliss, John. *Pioneers to the West.* Children's True Stories: Migration. Chicago: Heinemann-Raintree, 2012.

Fitzgerald, Michael Oren, ed. *Children of the Tipi: Life in the Buffalo Days.* Bloomington, Ind.: Wisdom Tales, 2013.

Gunderson, Jessica. *Your Life as a Pioneer on the Oregon Trail.* The Way It Was. Mankato, Minn.: Picture Window Books, 2012.

INTERNET SITES

FactHound offers a safe, fun way to find Internet sites related to this book. All of the sites on FactHound have been researched by our staff.

Here's all you do:

Visit *www.facthound.com*

Type in this code: 9781476540610

Super-cool stuff!

Check out projects, games and lots more at
www.capstonekids.com

CRITICAL THINKING USING THE COMMON CORE

1. How did horses make life easier for people living on the Plains? (Key Ideas and Details)

2. Look at the sidebar "Black Blizzards" on page 16. What is the author trying to explain in this sidebar? (Craft and Structure)

INDEX